Grabbing the Apple:
An Anthology of New York
Women Poets

Cover design © 2016 Janine DiNatale

All rights reserved. No portion of this publication may be reproduced, stored in a retrieval system, or transmitted in any form or by any means, electronic, mechanical, photocopying, or recording without the prior written permission of Terri Muuss and MJ Tenerelli unless such copying is expressly permitted by federal copyright law. Address inquiries to Permissions, JB Stillwater Publishing, 12901 Bryce Court NE, Albuquerque, NM 87112.

Library of Congress Cataloging-in-Publication Data

20160409
JB Stillwater Publishing Company
12901 Bryce Avenue NE
Albuquerque, NM 87112
Jbstillwater.com
Printed in the United States of America

I am the Pronoia of the pure light; I am the thought of the undefiled spirit...

Eve to Adam, The Gnostic Apocryphon of John

Foreword:

This collection is a labor of love. This collection is also a labor of necessity. In response to the glaring lack of parity for women in the arts, we decided to create a space for women's voices. Women telling women's stories. Here in New York, women have been breathing new life into poetry, a literary genre long dominated by men. As New Yorkers and poets ourselves, we live in the midst of these dazzling, sometimes forgotten voices and knew we wanted to celebrate them.

In its nascent stages, we had no idea how this collection would ultimately come together. What we received overwhelmed us. The love, the fury, the wit, the strength of so many astounding women's voices, each one unique but bound to the others by place. New York—there's nowhere like it, and oh, how these poets represent. The energy, savvy, wisdom and power of the New York woman emanates from these poems, both individually and as a collection.

The story of Eve has been, more often than not, interpreted by men. Eve has been presented as greedy, lustful, disobedient and ignorant. But what if Eve were the real hero and mother of us all? Where would we be had she never looked for knowledge, asked the important questions, challenged the powers that be? None of us exist but for her bravery and quest to know more, to push the envelope and, by extension, help us all grow bolder. The women in this collection are equally bold. Not content to have their story told for them, they grab the apple with both hands and tell it themselves. We couldn't be prouder to be a part of this telling and encourage you, our reader, to boldly grab hold and take a bite.

M.J. Tenerelli and Terri Muuss
The Editors

Contents:

Part I | EDEN

Iris N. Schwartz	3	In Morocco
Mindy Kronenberg	4	Veiled
Emma Rose	5	Lilith
Gabriella Belfiglio	6	Unbecoming
Michelle Whittaker	7	Predator
Jennifer Magliano	8	Air and All the Elements
Karla Linn Merrifield	11	Because a Gig was Hard to Come by in 1933
Kate Boning Dickson	12	love, lamp
Barbara Ann Branca	13	Baby Boom Room
Joan Vullo Obergh	15	Anniversary Ritual at Pinelawn
Hala Alyan	16	Even Fevers Make Bodies

Part II | THE FALL

Linda Kleinbub	19	Like That of the Purple Orchid in My Garden
Gladys Henderson	20	Rope Dancers
Jeanne Dickey	21	Lunch
Jane LeCroy	22	Salmonella Cinderella
Lisa Freedman	23	God of Spokes
Dd. Spungin	26	Chapped Hands
Linda Simone	27	Rara Avis
Sue Allen	28	Lotus Feet
Maggie Berke	29	At Night
Meagan Brothers	30	Location x 3
Wendy Galgan	32	Penelope
Stacy Santini	34	Edie
Vicki Iorio	36	Crossing Over
Liv Mammone	37	The Blind Date

Sharon Bourke	40	Thin Walls	
Muriel Harris Weinstein	41	Caught in a Spider's Web	
Karen Jakubowski	42	Bruised Fruit	
Pramila Venkateswaran	43	The Rapist's Wife	
Teri Coyne	45	100 Rapes	
Pramila Venkateswaran	47	The Long Shadow of Evil	

Part III | AFTER THE GARDEN

Hala Alyan	51	Listen,
Karen Schulte	53	Telling Our Stories
Barbara Southard	54	Mothers of the Dead Children Society
Barbara Reiher-Meyers	55	Youngest of Seven
Harriet Pasca-Ortgies	56	What is Left
Stella Padnos-Shea	57	It Started
Miriam Stanley	59	Dina
Deborah Hauser	60	In April
R.A.K.	61	Recovered Memory ABC's
Kate Kelly	62	Hard Rain
Wanda Schubmehl	63	Acorns
Gloria g. Murray	65	Penis Envy
Kelly J. Powell	66	Stained Glass Prison
Terri Muuss	68	Polished Dimes
Maggie Bloomfield	70	Sex
Anita S. Pulier	71	Feng Shui in 13E
Nancy Keating	73	The Grammar of Higher Learning
M.J. Tenerelli	75	A Woman in My Poems

Thanks and Acknowledgments	77
About the Editors	79
About the Cover Artist	83
Contributor Biographies	84

PART I | EDEN

Iris N. Schwartz

In Morocco

I sell truth for pigeons,
Bake them into pigeon pies—
Fold in almonds for purity,
Cinnamon for strength.

Keep one treat for myself,
Trade four to women in Rabat.
Outside our homes,
We swoop into the pies
In time for scent of oranges
To rush in,
Wrap us tight with hope,
Keep us steady as trees,

Until a new flock visits—
As my sisters and I bake
In ancient heat and
Spring for avian feathers
In the blue.

Mindy Kronenberg

Veiled

The fabric on her scarf is threaded
beige and gold, glinting as she tilts
her head from notebook to my desk,
shyly lifting dark eyes as she read
her poems aloud, the words like

blossoms caught in a wind, spinning
above us, splitting into petals
that scatter like fading song.
She is from Punjab, but I see Chagall
in the maidens that float from her page--

first dancing in love, then churning in dreams,
then hung upside down, caught in a vortex
of blood and clouds, unraveled but silenced.
She curls before me as she reads, singing
of soul, body, desire, the veil that burns.

Emma Rose

Lilith

Of apples, the Winesap rolls down to the place of the king,
why! I see only the dark smooth surface, the wine peel

of the fruit when the apple whirls out from the blue-space,
the non-space where things wait invisible to take their turn

in the lives of people. The apple appears when least expected
for the luscious art – the sweet nectar of loving, so deeply

forgotten, is jarred away on the unreachable shelves of
memory like a Buddha, the smiling white alabaster image

of the saint, this a heart of higher order, not the usual
banquet of guests feasting but love for the seasoned traveler.

Last summer was where I found him sitting under the tree ripe
with fruit and our hearts like wolf puppies ravenous with love.

We play cards and in solitaire become a team to mount our
horses on the same side of the river banks and slay the jacks

to bring in the aces and the Queen! She who befriends us
walks with serpents in her shoes and is not afraid of the wild,

she lives in trees, where swords clatter on shields and blood
soaks the sand, her lips wrapped dry round her aching teeth.

Her hair is a trail, the jeweled night she drags behind, a silver
crescent under the arm where a snake coils to bite her own tail.

The harvest this year, the deep wine of apples hangs seductively
from the branches like Lilith watching us through the tree hole.

Gabriella Belfiglio

Unbecoming

This morning, I reach
for a clementine
in the bottom of the crate
only to feel a squish
in my palm. I lift it out
but instead of chucking it
into the compost, I look--
the way the mold has taken
over, replacing orange:
fuzzy white with highlights of green.

How Zen, I think, this relinquish
to soft, this pelagic release
into decay. A canvas
offering the craters of mold
to be exposed. I imagine
myself, a piece of fruit,
an aphasic rot. No *greater* purpose,
no rent to pay, no one to wait for,
no emails to answer.
Only this placid undoing.

Michelle Whittaker

Predator

This story barely to begin does not die yet—
Wait.
for the last appendage, man slow smoking
his snake—
Wait—
for the sweating egress—
and
Later, in a lake, in a slake lake, the bluest girl—

Jennifer Magliano

Air & All the Elements
    for Joyce

Fire

No shelter, noontime sun.
You are barefoot standing,
scalded feet
head hatless
tenting your babies.
Wild hair warning
of a fire higher
than high noon,
mightier
than all the heartless blazes
set in your path.

Water

Waves, an undulating
wall behind you.
A gray, unsettled skyline of
throbbing warfare.
You swam from there
though belongings beckoned
from your sunken ship.

Now your toes touch,
your smile breaks the surface
and you gather shells
you've never seen.

Imagine: tides can give
what you ask and deliver
your banishments
back to the water,
smoothing that sea
to the skyline, the sheet
of a new bed
you bought for yourself.

Earth

Long legs like
a pair of swans
on water, you glide
over land.
Laughter trumpets
and you are
your own mate
for life.

Once our legs swung
like any child's
in any chair--
before gravity
grabbed us,
urged our grounding
so we'd stand up to

anything

and you did
oh you did.

These years have sewn us
to the giving ground
with bloody, sacred stitches

that stretch to allow
for skydiving:
A pair of white swans
in takeoff. a trumpet call
of joy--your namesake
and your birthright.

Karla Linn Merrifield

Because a Gig Was Hard to Come by in 1933

In younger days, JoJo the poet lucked out
for she always did like to hobnob with the filthy
rich and famous so when Marjorie and E. F.
employed her as laureate of their yacht, of course,
JoJo said yes, so what if she had to sleep
in servants' quarters in the hold and once
in a while babysit Dina Merrill, daughter-princess
of the uniformed crew of seventy-two.
JoJo the Poet took her consolations in poems
made under full sail in the master's stateroom.

Kate Boning Dickson

love, lamp

dear bulb
I'm tired
of indulging
your demands
the way you fill
your electric desire
through me
not wired for this
I'm drained
from completing
your circuit

weary of snapping
to attention
when in a lovely shadow reverie
I'm numb from hearing
the persistence
of your hum

I like long nights
in darkness--
prefer the subtle brilliance
of a slow dawn
but still you twist in me
and I can't resist
the power of your need

Barbara Ann Branca

Baby Boom Room

In here, I hear
voices of children past.

Here, old woman in the shoe room,
see the post war boom room,
now I know my A B

See the suburbs grow room,
before the sprawl before the mall room.
From this Great Spirit Manitou hill,
have a plain view of the Hempstead plain.
We learned *O Beautiful for Spacious Skies*--
big with giraffe clouds and Howdy Doody faces,
long dead Matinecocks in moccasins.
We drank two-cent milk out of glass bottles
from Matinecock dairy with a picture,
a healthy white boy bursting
his buttons with good health.

The dairy was up on a hill.
Where is the hill now?
Where are the Matinecocks?

This very room of spacious skies
divided in two, the quiet
girls learned Dick, Jane and Sally
from newly printed readers.
We learned to raise our hands, wait
our turn, form a line. We uncovered
truths. The art teacher came in with crayons

and rough white paper.
Draw children draw.
I couldn't find a purple crayon. I colored
my tulips blue and Mother laughed for years
about blue tulips. See Junie, Karen and Joanne
From original old dark houses, not like the rest
of us in ticky tacky Levitt ranches and Cape Cods
built on potato farms. Larry made
his millions in real estate and Lynn is building habitat
for humanity... but Bobby in the front
row got messed up after Viet Nam
Run Bobby run
but not fast enough, caught dealing drugs,
served some hard time in Texas. Maida smart
as a whip, went to college straight from 11th grade,
became a doctor, discovered drugs
lives on a different hill now overlooking
San Francisco Bayand Patty-- she taught me how to snap
my fingers, how to play ball. She never threw
like a girl. She went to San Francisco, too, got herself
a penis and became Patrick.

We all graduated in paper gowns,
our grandmothers made, sang Patti Page's big
hit, *How much is that doggie
in the window? The one with the waggily tail-ail-ail-ail*
We topped the charts. We wagged our tails.
We found our voice
here in the baby boom room.

Joan Vullo Obergh

Anniversary Ritual at Pinelawn

She never finds him here
hitching up baggy twill pants,
a sweat-stained gardening shirt
that no longer does him proud;
never here crutched against a spade
catching his breath, mopping his brow;
not here ducking between row after row
of granite reminders pushing
through frost membranes
the way tender jonquil tips might be doing
had he still been planting them.
There is no trace—no scent—no memory
of him here.
And so she comes.

Hala Alyan

Even Fevers Make Bodies

Jerusalem springs forth like a violence
and I
    audacious sashay

her gulfing streets with twin wings on my shoulder.

    Mouth,
I have skin soft enough to catch you

and the pink below the needle—
rot, rot.

Pinned beneath opium eyes I pitched
myself across

    the Atlantic. Celtic music kept pace of our lungs.

Root, you microscopic, sly thing.

Even teethed by a lover my organs pulse for certain cities.

I saw a woman on a porch once. Her hair, silver as tusks,
    swung

polished in the simple Vienna light.

She said comets spin on these July
evenings

because Allah loves to dance in their
lovely glow.

PART II | THE FALL

Linda Kleinbub

Like that of the Purple Orchid in My Garden
a cento

The moon tonight is dazzling, is full.
In dreams I'm wild with guilt
entering the seawater at twilight
like Blake, naked in his garden.

I'd give anything for one more night
and part my lips with a globe,
be gentle with me, I'm new to this.
As dawn breaks, he enters.

I lay down in the tweed of one man
that first frost night
as in a children's book
composed entirely of snow.

Gladys Henderson

Rope Dancers

Our ride was slow on the black horse
your uncle said was from the circus.

I held you close; my hands circled your waist.
It was my first time on a horse.

Wind brought the taste of cattle dung,
plains were the color of dried blood.

Along the way the price of hardship,
bleached white bones in December sun.

Your words were bandaged, carefully chosen;
the horror of your truth paralyzed.

We rode as rope dancers, reins in hand,
trembling through your childhood.

I held on in terror, a frightened child, as we
traveled to the place you called home.

Jeanne Dickey

Lunch

Friendless in school
again. This time
will be different.
Snow drifts down clean,
becomes muddy
outside the dining hall. Inside,
I have a grilled cheese sandwich.
A girl I know from French class
whispers something about birth control,
then introduces me to her blue-eyed
friend. They're sleeping together
(she's told me) but he won't be more
than that, a friend:
the word that lies
like a tomato
on my grilled cheese sandwich
that will never be cake.

Jane LeCroy

Salmonella Cinderella

Salmonella Cinderella
She's the beast, he's the belle
He's the beau, she's the show
She says yes, he says no

Thinking king of hearts he is
She's the card right under his

I read your mind, never mind
Always your deck, never mine
Hours ours, for hours and hours
We go together like funeral & flowers

Lisa Freedman

God of the Spokes

God of the binary code,
why do you pulse on and
off
separating halves
dying for union?

God of the insulin pump I couldn't stand
attached always to my side
the sky blue pills -- five --
and the white and the burnt umber --
every morning, every night.

God of my nephew's inhaler –
his gasping, his steroids.
        Of treatments and side effects.

God of leveling shocks,
of Owen from the ferry, who smiled and read books
and could never tolerate
school.

God of Owen I saw pedaling home.
God of falling out of bed
hitting his head
and lying face down and still
until the cleaning woman came three days later.
        Of his red helmet hanging off the handle bars.

God of the blond boy on the pew, waiting for
his Uncle O.

God of the Saturday quiet before dawn before the clamor of pitches, practice,
and foot-longs with relish.

God of being there and of the questions that comfort
and disappoint like home.
My mother, two blades
of one scissor, shearing the world into
tight lips or smiles
chores or happy hours
Dad's home or Dad's not here
        Of Mom's winked code, invisible revolutions.

God of the big scoops of dirt
crumbling along the top of Owen's casket.
His messenger bag and his cell phone

all the people he spoke to
while we crossed the harbor.
God of the shovel left upright in the earth.
The sweat, the giving away,
grief like garlic, like thorns, the scald and the scar.

God of these sweltering steps, the humid heels
sinking through grass into soft soil from
the gravesite to the limo.

God of revelation.
This man's face
an invitation.
This friend of Owen, friend of mine
with hands that press into the small of my back
after the funeral.
        Of the unbreathing silence, the fear.

I have to say
I have
AIDS.

God of the pouring down drive
the secrets our stories the comfort
of windshield wipers of tissues
fingertips and lips.

      Of the majesty of now.

Dd. Spungin

Chapped Hands

Chapped hands cry blood
Beg, please, no water
but dishes need washing and the heat's off
Your breath frosts the one window not broken
and the baby cries, doesn't know
she's not supposed to be this cold
Your hands cry with her as your heart breaks
like the windows, smashed by anger.

Chapped hands lift her up, cradle her
to your cold, fingerprinted neck
She doesn't know it should feel warm and soft
You look at kitchen knives with lust,
dream of rat poison and escape
but it's too cold to run
and baby's asleep
It's quiet, cold and quiet--
for now.

Linda Simone

Rara Avis

It's March and it's morning
and not even the pyrotechnics
of Times Square can cut the chill.
Pigeon-prints score
concrete oval like a Chinese scroll.
At the base, tall, ten-

gallon hat perched on his blond head,
boots and spurs,
BVDs -- the Naked Cowboy

nothing else 'cept some tats, a *gui*-tar,
and his neon grin.
Crowds like homing pigeons.

Two ladies in rabbit and cashmere
preen for him. A teen
in tartan and bagpipes
points her cell phone, snaps.

His left hand
cups some tourist ass.
Who would believe?

Pick the right plot of asphalt
drop your seeds
and out fly your bare-skinned dreams.

Sue Allen

Lotus Feet

Flower heart hurts
    gathering fragrance
Tight bind buds smaller feet
Break bend and bleed into
    hidden love treasure
Object of awe

On the 6th day of the 6th Lunar month
Parades of 3 inch lily shoes
    float violent desire
Apparitions of rotting flesh
Pungent powder rises from the dust
    of smooth folded petal fetish

Lifeless girl ghost pale behind her curtain
    wears silk slippers to bed
Embroidered pillow cushions feet
    that fit in hands

A thousand years of madness
    for flowered heels so high
Mythical raft revolves like the moon
A drunk dreams of five pearls
    tossing lotus seeds at passing stars

Golden ball strikes silver swan
Plum pit replaces grape seed
Vine wrappings loosen,
    then grip young maiden
Her hooves held in merchant's palm

Maggie Berke

At Night

I am strut and the lengths
of hemlines getting shorter.
I am head held high and eyes
getting stronger. I am curved sculpture—
milk white woman, desert,
consumption, there only for eyes
turned up from grit
as the click of my heels saunter past.

I am uncomfortable eye contact,
legs made for tongues,
words dripping with sweat—
sex bombs at my feet.
I am a doll woman.
Touch my plastic parts.
I am up-turned neck, see through
veins, vulnerable to hands that
hold down.

I don't want to wait for the buzzards
picking apart a carcassed soul.
Don't look at me.
I don't want your eyes, unless they are in my hands.
I don't want you to cry when I cut my hair.
I am not Rapunzel.

If I am ever locked up
alone in a tower, it is only
to get away from
men like you.

Meagan Brothers

Location x 3

where are we now?
every poem should
set the scene:
exterior nighttime – bewilderment.
I'm in the city,
you're in the living room.
in a few hours, I'll be at work
thinking of a purpose
(but there never is a purpose)
(no wait, I remember – the purpose is
  money.)

set the scene:
interior nighttime --
would it make any difference
if we added more trees?
if we turned sixth avenue
into a cul-de-sac?
no matter where we are
there is always
wanting,
the distant breath of lives
we haven't steered toward.
everywhere we go
there is the sticky pulse of doubt,
the hasty attempts to
restage the play.
all of our friends are here
and we are careless as youth
pretending we don't know or don't care

about nuclear fallout or subway bombs,
pretending cancer won't settle in our bones
or a sexless chill
won't drape itself upon us.

where are we now?
in a desperate dance
that has no steps
in a holding pattern
trying to circle back home.

set the scene:
even without really moving
something has shifted.
we tried to keep still
but we move like sand moves
when the wind pushes against us,
hard and invisible and
in infinitesimal fragments.
we find ourselves redrawn
into lines that look the same
but are always waving further
away from shore.

Wendy Galgan

Penelope

Foolish old man.
"No one knew me but my dog,
and he was dying" my ass.
I knew Odysseus
from his first footfall
outside my door.

But still, it's his story.
So I duck my head and smile,
looking up through my veil of hair
only if the bright-eyed goddess
shares our table.

Athena grins as
my man of
twists and turns
describes himself awash
in the goddess's disguise.
Old rags and a bad toupee
is more like it,
enough to fool a bunch of men
and a barely bearded boy.

I didn't need to hear his bowspring
quiver as he passed
to know my own husband.
To know the smell of him,
musk and sea breeze and tall grasses,
as he stepped through the doorway.

Still, I understood the game.
So I ignored my heartbeat,
feigned indifference
as he spun his tale of news
from other shores.
Pretended not to notice as he paused,
one hand lifted toward me,
before he left to join the suitors
and start his deadly game.

I called for crisp bed linens,
sweet wine and fresh figs.
I bathed, perfumed my hair,
sat beside our marriage bed,
itself as rooted to this house as I,
while Odysseus and Telemachus,
husband and son, man and boy,
bathed my house in blood.

Stacy Santini

Edie

I drip ego into lashes dark
as coal. I paint my mask for hours eating
reds and blues, smoking
to the filter - another
and another
finger flesh tar mixing my paint
Warhol's whore, his muse
I am skeletal
broken and spread
on Campbell Soup dribbled floors – my gap
open, staring
from crinkled mirrors
bouncing from tin foiled
walls.

*I want more of it all. I want
so much of it, of that
more, more, more.*

I am my chandelier earrings
my limousine
the celebrated black leotard goat
I am Bellevue
I am Fuzzy my father
who sculpted his desire into my youth
every inch of my learning
under the glaze of his longing
femme fatale, just like a woman....
I break like a little girl
I get poked
amphetamines driving my way

And it is never
enough.
*I want more of it all. I want
so much of it, of that
more, more, more*
Dr. Roberts gets it
Ondine gets it
Nico gets it
Andy gets it
Ginsberg gets it
and we all get it
and give each other it over and over
in the back room of Max's Kansas City
in the Chelsea Hotel
in The Factory
in the alleyways
on Dylan's farm
we give it to each other everywhere
laughing
screaming
till I am only legs
90 inch legs plied apart
dig That
spread wide
pinned down on that silver floor
because I am a star
his star
drilling, writhing
speed pumping
now everyone's star

gone
thank you Patti Smith for remembering
that I knew how to dance
and that I was so much more.

Vicki Iorio

Crossing Over

Wire down on Sixth Ave
can't get across the street
where Rite Aid keeps my antidepressants

I stay in my apartment on hot weekends
with my medicated cocktails
I've picked up Moby Dick again
my college copy   dead fish stiff and yellow

My college lover's tongue
tasted like peppermints
his major was animal husbandry
he became a dairy farmer in upstate New York

I could have been the wife of a dairy farmer
last week when I went to the fortune teller
she gave me back my money
closed my palm and made the sign of the cross

I can't shake off the feeling that zombies
are following me it's the antidepressants
my therapist says

She says the new dosage will take some time to kick in
if I could get across Sixth Avenue
I could start the dosage
but the fucking wire is too big
for the chronically depressed to cross over

Liv Mammone

The Blind Date

You know, maybe you should have them
cut off your legs and give
you those cool metal ones.
That might be better for you.
Analyze his voice. The way it curves

against his tobacco stained
teeth. Sip your Coke before responding.
Decide he isn't joking. Let the cold
bite of burger roll in your
mouth. Swallow hard.
Consider what you know.

He's the first responder on
e-spin-the-bottle.com;
spends weeks begging for a set
of topless photos
which you take at 4AM
in dingy webcam light.

He video chats, his seven
inch penis with its skinned,
oblong head like a vulture.
You do not want it inside you
but you want him to want it

inside you—you are fifteen
and this past Christmas your uncle, vodka
spilling his voice all over the kitchen table,
promised a prostitute

for your eighteenth birthday--
won't let you grow up without

feeling a man's hand and you're scared.
Scared your body is already a
haunted house ready for the wrecking ball.
So you stand on the good foot,
stomach pressed against the bathroom sink,
curling your hair with four fingers.

Your right hand is useless as chopsticks for soup,
your right foot a blackened fork curling in on itself.
Under your peasant blouse, you sweat with effort.
 Before he signed off that morning, he called you
beautiful but when you open the door
he smells of smoke and BO.
His hair hangs like tangled clam nets.
He has no plan, asks you where to eat.

Then he is pulling to the side of the road and
you know. And you have to explain
that your body is a lock box;
that without time your crooked
thighs will make a pocket knife of him.
He will break all the springs in you.

He looks at your crutches in his trunk and says,
Just don't make me wait too long.
You want to take off your jeans
and hurl them, balled up like snakeskin,
into his backseat with the Big Gulp cups
and Cheetos bags. You want to apologize
for how early you were born,
sorry the doctors even bothered to save you.

Now you're sitting in a dusty diner, a block
from your house where the neon signs have
long since short circuited
trying to figure out
why he won't order food--
why he won't look at you.

The vinyl seat screeches under him
The greasy fries are an audience
in front of you. You've eaten off your glittered
lip gloss. He is twisting his body. His eyes
move like mosquitoes. Under the table, your
knees pop. Did he hear them?

You know, maybe you should have them
cut off your legs and give
you those cool metal ones.
That might be better for you.

He is as earnest as a drunk uncle over
strains of Nat King Cole.
Drink your Coke.
String together a laugh
from the syllables choking your throat.

Don't tell him there is metal in your marrow;
that you have plates instead of ankle bones.
Don't tell him your high school was
a hospital bed; a classroom with morphine walls.
Instead, say you want to go home.

There, you'll sit on the couch for another three hours,
your mother folding laundry, as he shows you
his favorite NASCAR crashes on VHS
while you think about metal and flesh;
while your skin burns.

Sharon Bourke

Thin Walls

Don't raise your voice.
Don't break that bottle.
Don't slash her face.
Don't take her life.

In this night of the power failure,
when ice is on the wires
and wind seeps under the door,
people burn candles,
and drink whiskey,

listen—
to how you sound.

Muriel Harris Weinstein

Caught In A Spider's Web

Each morning she finds
her arms wound so tightly around
herself, rose colored blotches
tattoo her upper arm,

Damp, still in heat,
a clammy dew perforates
her empty night. She looks
at him with hate and longing

He lies alongside her
rigid, in a jute cocoon.
She presses herself against him
but his wrapping tightens.

She studies his jaw, pointed
like the wooden beards of Pharaohs,
his lips, thin wires,
pulled tight as winches.

He houses himself in a cage,
his hands folded at the elbow
doesn't care to extend them
unbend them to welcome or caress.

She wonders, why can't she move…
why is she still there?

Karen Jakubowski

Bruised Fruit

One month after
the apple appeared
above my elbow
on my right arm
perfect and round,
delivered in my sleep;

One month after
it rotted from red to purple
then black and indigo
finally fading from yellow to flesh;

One month after
co-workers' backward glances
changed from concern
to get the job done;

One month after
my boss asked me to close the door
to tell me *we support you;*

One month after
the shame faded
to just another secret
I tried to run from;

One month after
my boss asked *what's wrong.*
Is your husband still...

I answered *not at the moment.*

Pramila Venkateswaran

The Rapist's Wife

Do you know if he raped that girl?
You are all screaming for his head.
The person whose head you want
is my *patidev*, understand, he is good to me,
he cares for our Chintu, do you know
he is a great father, a provider, his father
lives with us and he takes the old man
to Doctor *saab*? People marching in Delhi
scream like hyenas,
you reporters breaking my door wanting
answers, do you really know he
raped that girl, she must be lying, these modern
girls will say anything for attention,
why would he do that, he works
all day so he can send us money
he wouldn't do this, it's too horrible,
bilkul galath, galath, galath, he was not
anywhere near her, must have been
someone else, you people think
we are alike, we are poor so you
don't care, just catch hold
of some miserable fool, hound him,
bas, khatam, you're done.
All this screaming at my door
as if you want to strip me of my
life, my husband, how will we live
without him, have you thought of this,
when you keep asking me questions
your camera lens in my face,
you *shaitan*, monsters, fucking

sons of bitches tearing my life, flinging
my entrails all over the news?

Teri Coyne

100 Rapes

Long after the treaties were signed
and the mud had crusted around the soles of the soldiers boots
I hid in the doorway of the charred remains of my Baba's
dress shop
and watched them in the café smoking and reading the papers.

I saw the one who smelled like straw and vinegar
who said fucking a goat was better than me
he drank his coffee black and in one gulp
and teased the monkey man
who made me lay on my stomach and burned me with
matches.
They laugh about the old days.
The rape camps.
The carnage of spirit.
The way they made ghosts out of girls.

It would be impossible to catch them all,
Nadia tells me when she finds me
quivering in the hallway
unable to barter my memory for sleep.
You must go on, she says.
They do.

When the cigarettes and coffee are gone
the men return to their wives and goats
and thank their God for the mercy he has shown them.

I wait until daylight bleeds into the blacktop
that conceals the scar cracked road that dragged me away.

I follow the crumbs of cobblestone
past the park where my father carried me on his shoulders
back to the boarding house
where I pay for my room with my body.
I count the steps
like I counted the rapes.
One...two...three
and pray I get home
before I reach one hundred.

Pramila Venkateswaran

The Long Shadow of Evil

The hall spins, bride, groom, flowers,
guests, husband. Then routine happens.

Do I have all the ingredients
for the feast?

A bird bangs itself against glass and falls.
That's how his hand against my face.

Spirit, better not stand me up, I yell
silently. This is how surprise springs and settles,

wordless bitterness in my throat,
his causeless rage twisting him ugly.

I know the difference between sinking dark
and womb dark: My marriage is dung,

I choke, marriage is dung dung dung.
Singers croon *sitakalyanam vaibogame*

Rama kalyanam vaibogame
as bride and groom walk around the fire.

Roses on the nuptial bed, stitched into garlands,
roses perfuming waters anointing the wedded pair.

I place my hands on my truth-telling heart
thud-thud thud-thud, I close my eyes, the hall spins.
His rage, my humiliation, then the pretense,

laughter and gossip, the rippling of everafter,

symbols of fertility mocking me: twin hills of lentils,
clay pots filled with new sprouts, babies

placed on the bride's silken lap, the circle
of fire redrawing her womb.

My husband's father and his father's father,
their anger, a fiery chain, dogs my sons.

How will they pick their paths
through evil sown by ghosts?

My dead mother calls, *Sitala, tune up the strings,
before your mind dulls and bells drag you to duties.*

His vying words, I'll-die-and-only-then-
you-will-regret, I tune out.

Mother visits in dreams, Sing your heart out,
you're wedded to words till your tongue is ash.

PART III | THE GARDEN

Hala Alyan

Listen,

she says,
your hands might be cold but the sun will reach us

soon. Five decades ahead of me,

she finds certain accessories trifling: gloves, cigarettes,
hairbrush. Hamsa necklace

and a plate decorated with hieroglyphics,
this is tea.

An Egyptian suitor, she laughs, many years ago,

asked her to marry by the Red Sea.
And then a Moroccan, two Iraqis. Her with sepia hair

and a face like porcelain.

She sighs. It was ruin to be loved
like that, waking to desert

hyacinths
and lace gowns sewn by deft Parisian fingers.

Almonds crunch between our teeth as the *muezzin* begins.

From the ascent,
she points to the hill where a prophet knelt

to touch soil.

I ask about the lace, if it itched. No, she muses, but the
roses

always brought beetles and a rash.

When she finally wed,
it was a farmer's son, poor, but with kind eyes and hands

that always smelled of oranges.
Listen, she scolds,

enough of this heartbreak talk. Drink your tea.

In the winter she would boil
jasmine, dozens of petals at once, and dip her hair

slowly in the steam. Listen,
she says,

her eyes suddenly
serious, he might be dead but not loving anyone

else won't bring him back.

Her wedding night, she and the farmer's son made love
like bread,

her voice rising with her body.
This was Jaffa,

1946, and they kept the window open, for the air,
for the moon.

Karen Schulte

Telling Our Stories
   for Janet

We all live in magic circles
until we don't, my dear friend said,
in her mourning clothes,
as if this was a secret between us,
as if we were the only ones telling our stories—

a beginning without an end,
a moving kaleidoscope floating images,
dipping into legend and repetition
much like the circle the bee makes

moving over purple sage testing
its sweet sap before dipping in
the pale violet of the long stem
lavender never moving far
from where he began flower to flower,

the same as waves disappear
under their own roar to find
deeper water rising again,
a force much like our lives
and the tales we tell
in uneven margins as

sheets of paper birch bleed
white on serried edges,
our stories are our own
and each other's told until
there is no breath left to do
much more than continue...

Barbara Southard

Mothers of the Dead Children Society

Like born-again Christians, members of self-help groups,
secret cells of anarchists, addicts, vegetarians, atheists,

mothers of dead children can spot each other in a crowded
room.

Each mother can tell you how a clay pot can shatter on the
stone floor,
how she pieces together one small shard with another,

glues them together until the pot is strong enough to hold
water.

Barbara Reiher-Meyers

Youngest of Seven

left behind, entangled in the web
guarded by an angry virgin
and I, the least and weakest
watched as one by one they fled.
silken strings of ennui
wrapped, entrapped, encircled,
in the 50's culture dome.
Mother, how I miss you

Harriet Pasca-Ortgies

What is Left

You in your floral apron,
stretching sections of dough end to end,
forming just the right thickness,
floured hands coaxing the soft mass
into a perfect circle.
Curling it between your fingers,
you line the deep dish
to receive sugar-coated apples,
dash of nutmeg,
sprinkling of lemon.

I pull your rolling pin from the drawer,
trace of green on its aging handle,
my movements -- too abrupt --
the pieces stick
pull up, leave holes.
I try to smooth the broken
fragments, hoping it will
be good enough.

Stella Padnos-Shea

It Started

and the end was beginning.
The intravenous was locked into my right
arm. I wore the hospital smock
flounced with doves, my panties long gone.
At first it was easy, a cake walk,
a drinking game, the bumps
on the screen barely born,
like we all were
once. I just lay back,
yes, I'm fine, honey.

In the middle of the night
the jokes were subsiding,
the abstract enemy of pain
was introducing himself fast.
Memories go in and out like desire.
I remember climbing onto
the hospital bed, on all fours,
the voice of the kindly nurse,
Baby, you can't be climbin'
on the bed like that.

I'll never recognize her face,
I am long gone for her, as well.
One killer pain came, which was not
fierce enough. I'd settle into imaginary sleep,
startle awake, beginning with a low moan.
I was no different from
any other animal then,
a low moan being born
somewhere in my body.

Somehow seconds and hours were passing,
the night was still darkly lit in fabulous Brooklyn.
The gaudy sun was on show
when the pain changed;
it was time to push.
A part of my body had to come out.
I was mistakenly in charge. Can you believe
the doctor was serious when he said,
I see black hair.

Minutes later, those condensed,
super-real minutes later, I was handed
a person. This is your open
baby from your open body.
It was only the beginning.

Miriam Stanley

Dina

A baby carved out at forty.
Cancerous breasts at fifty.
Later, the solar plexus cracked like a lobster.
Surgeons sew the aorta under a rubbery grip;
masks, scarves—blue-green, aquatic linen under chilly light.
The family pacing in pairs in their imaginary ark.

Later, you return to work, bitching about parking spaces, time
wasted, the silver hair shorn for a quick morning routine.
The milk white scan of morning report.
Your salt taste of impertinence, slipping out of meetings at
wide-angled noon.
The world under close inspection.
Ultrasound, six months, checking for fear.

You stay up at night: a pill waiting to dissolve.
The repairs future/past – a mobile of knives.
You spoon a husband back from a long separation.
Entertain dying in his arms;
a silver lining of relapse.

His muscles lean ovals holding tight.
His eyes red sunken living rooms.
A witness of what you were.
The skin flap cut from the belly, pirated onto the chest,
everything corporal moves in time.

The Buddhists say the only
thing constant is change.
We just want to hold the pieces.
You kiss that man's baldhead.
Fall into blindness: a doll.

Deborah Hauser

In April

I plant a flat of impatiens in the yard
creating color where the day before
there was only dirt and feel lighter all day

until I read in the evening paper
about farmers down in Florida
warming orange groves

with electric heat, but the trees
won't respond to artificial light
and the fruit dries up

like the breast of a mother
grieving her stillborn child
because sometimes it snows in April

and the crops fail
and my womb is too bruised
for anything to take root within it.

I stop reading, fold the paper
into quarters, cut one orange
tulip, place it in a vase on the kitchen table

and remind myself it isn't safe
to plant until after Mother's Day.

R.A.K

Recovered Memory ABC's

Albert
behind
closed
doors
excuses
facades
guises
hair-washing
innuendoes
Jenny
kissing
lascivious
me?
No.
overt
pushing
quietly
risky
secrets
tickling
underhanded
vexed
why?
x-rated
youth
zoned out

Kate Kelly

Hard Rain

knowing all there is to know
must be an awful burden
cloud said to earth
as it passed overhead dulling the day
and because you have heard me
we're in this together
and if they get me
they'll get you too

(the cloud was not kidding)

earth turned her soft belly of silt to the sky
and answered the cloud's warning
with mustered up courage
she directed the cloud
to lay down her gun
on the table between them
walk away now
before it gets ugly

(the earth was pleading)

but cloud
thick with anger and frustration
stood her ground
and poured
and poured
and poured
a hard rain
down

Wanda Schubmehl

Acorns

When I was small,
we laid acorns into baskets of grass
and set them upon the river.
The wind blew
in all directions,
and made a sound of fire
burning all the grass and acorns
in the fields.
And the acorns we liberated
sailed in their grass baskets
past the conflagration on into the sea.
The world burned,
but the acorn-baskets
spun on silver currents,
finding their own way.
This was the first ending of the world.

When I was grown, we harnessed clouds,
pulling them behind tall gray horses
with manes of ice. The winter manes
lifted and fell with the horses' steps,
and the clouds rode the horses and the manes.
All the world disappeared in fog,
and the cloud-riders shouted
with the voices of the ancients,
who awoke and cried out,
so that the rocks tumbled down.
This was the second ending of the world.

Now I am old, and the silence of stone
surrounds us. The valleys taste of acorns
and the mountains smell of fog.
We are the third ending of the world,
which dies quietly in its woven basket.
Horses lift it from the water
and blow their breath.
This is the first beginning
of the world.

Gloria g. Murray

Penis Envy

I watch them on a summer's day
hauling bricks or wooden crates
spreading tar across the avenue
hanging out of cranes
spitting into air
in sweaty tee shirts
and turned around baseball caps
the way they swat bees
the way they eat with mustard
dripping down their straggly beards
the way they swagger in tight jeans
and mud streaked boots
or in elegant pin striped suits
with spit shined shoes
leaving trails of musk and after shave
the way they unzip themselves
behind graffiti painted buildings
or overgrown bushes
as if there was never any question
the world was created
in seven days
just for them

Kelly J. Powell

Stained Glass Prison

> *As long as we're together*
> *With the moonlight shining—*
> *It doesn't matter what I did*
> *It doesn't matter what I did.*
>
> *Meema (Allie)*
> *5 East South, Suffolk County Correctional Center*

The girls have all gone out to yard—
to walk endless circles. T-shirts
hiked and rolled up become bikinis

cover a blacktop beach.
It's the ordinary things will break
your heart. Coughing, menstruating,

struggling for soap, utensils,
shampoo, shoes for the shower. Trade
backrubs for coffee and cosmetics—all these

girl things still so important here.
A bit of lotion, chapstick, hair ties torn
from standard issue socks.

Smells of coconut linger. Male guard
watches them shower from his booth.

Scrub whites in the sink, saving bleach
and plastic bags—tampon strings
shape eyebrows—are made into rings.

Barbecue sauce made from
leftover ketchup
discarded mustard
a stolen onion
a hoarded tomato.
Woven mats of old news cover
toilet seats, peanut butter packets
warmed between our hands.

Girl on suicide watch walks by in her green
velcro dress, head held high with her 24-hour guard.
At night you can hear them singing,
screaming, banging their heads
against cement walls withdrawing from crack,

heroin, heterosexuality. Masturbating, praying.
Sergeant makes his rounds.

Moonlight shines through
an open iron window grate
divine light
shape of chain mail
and cathedrals hits the floor
near beds chained to prison bars
on names scratched everywhere-
even in the soap.

Night fades and its morning.
Slowly familiar birdsong begins—cacophony
of a single bird strong enough
to nest on this roof.

Sun rises, presents herself
to everyone, everywhere equally
on prisons of our own making.

Terri Muuss

Polished Dimes

In a shadow under naked
staircase, we were poised for
ignition: a moonset kiss, our
thighs catching air under wind

blown skirts. Our bodies
shared an astonishing
arithmetic, infinite
versions of colored

stones. We came closer
than reaching—falling into
the precipice of holy. My head—
eels writhing in a bucket,

the faltering voice of our
"yes." She led me into
sparks of late
sun, blew my thoughts –

a thousand dandelion tufts
over a golden valley
of lips, palms, breasts, labia—
opening, burning through

cotton, wrists slicing icy
cataracts of milky seed pods,
swollen fruit, coming
over water, over fields,

the rushing rushing RUSHING, delirious
rain, smell of oxidizing metal. We fell
into the black of iris,
vortex of moan, thin white

leaves drawn on curtains, the hushed
night we held in our shaking
hands, until silence was too
loud—it seized the dress

of body we shared, its red
convoy of fish bones, bird
nests and drowsy
thorns. We lay in the arrow's quiver

after release—church doors flung
open on our pulsing— until
there was no sermon
left in our throats.

Maggie Bloomfield

Sex

Crabs mate face to face,
claws entwined,
eyes filled with the appearance
of strong feeling.
First, he dances
on pointy little claws
to lure the mature
female
onto her back,
both having shed their skins
at this point.
Exposed, vulnerable,
they clutch and buck and moan
like lovers everywhere.
the male peering
brainlessly into madam's eyes
with some crustacean impulse
of *I love her*
or
God, I want to pin her,
while, beneath him,
she muses primordially,
He's a terrible dancer
But I want to have his children.

Anita S. Pulier

Feng Shui in 13E

I am feeling reckless,
reading Kerouac,
studying Feng Shui,
leaving the toilet seat cover up

in an attempt
to allow bad Qi to escape
through NYC sewers.

Cannot recall
when I last cleaned the bowl.
Even the worst of Qi
may refuse my offer.

After checking
that the doorman is on duty
I open wide the front door.

Qi wafts through 13E
delighted with the absence
of locks and chains.

I run the water in the bathtub
creating a trickling fountain,
check my image in the

mirror now reflecting a
babbling brook, move furniture,
begin to understand the art

of relationships,

connectivity,
toilets, open doors,
water and reflecting mirrors,
all now rearranged,
setting the stage
for absolute bliss.

Then... nothing.
I hold vigil for the arrival
of inner peace.

Ambulance sirens scream,
neighbors shout,
children cry, dogs bark.

I watch you trip over the chair
I have just moved to allow
for the free movement of Qi.

While you curse,
I move the chair back to its spot,
turn off the water in the tub, re-chain the front door,

hope that Qi will give up on me,
allow me to get on with
muddling through,

an ancient art
I have spent years perfecting.

Nancy Keating

The Grammar of Higher Learning

Picked up a course catalog off a rack
and I knew right off it was for heaven

I'm a sucker for quadrangles and seminars and
redbrick Palladian libraries

my mother had worked at the local library
kind of day spa for knowledge

but here's God offering classes
with room and board and laundry all covered

and meals served up at the dining hall
and your only job is to study and learn

so I reached out to the Almighty and said
God do I have the right prerequisites

and she had such a magnificent throaty voice
and said you should know I don't care about those things

and I said can I test out of freshman comp
and she said in her thrilling contralto *Darlin'*

I always love being called Darlin'
It's like caramel pie but of course she knew that

my mother loved me dearly but with that reserved Irish love
God said *Darlin' your composition is perfect as is*

It was like God was giving me a big intellectual hug
and I was right there with her and one with everything

with all the universe vast and shimmering
and ineffably lovely in its interlocking parts

but then I had to ask the big question
God this totally sounds like smart-girl heaven

but I don't think I can swing the tuition
and she said *Darlin' you're all paid up*

M.J. Tenerelli

A Woman in My Poems

She flies off the ledge
Of a very tall building,
Her pink platforms beating her down
To the sidewalk below.
She is on fire in a stairwell.
She is crushed flat under the ceiling
Of the 94th floor.
She is saying goodbye on the desk phone
That still makes outgoing calls.
She is sitting under the desk
Saying the Lord's prayer 40 times,
In quick succession.
She's on a gurney, in a coffin, she's
One million tiny bits and fragments
Floating in the sun, out over the river.
She comes to me in a dream,
Perfectly put together
In an outfit she picked out
From Trash and Vaudeville.
She says, *This is how*
You should publish me.

Thanks and Acknowledgements:

Our deepest gratitude to Janet and Art Brennan of Casa De Snapdragon Publishing, Janine DiNatale, Matt Pasca, and all the women writers, poets, artists who submitted their work.

We are also forever indebted to the rich Long Island poetry community of which we are enthusiastically a part.

M.J. Tenerelli: I would like to thank my mama, Violet Sarah Veronica Tenerelli *nee* Hamil. She read me poetry instead of bedtime stories, and continued throughout her life to support my love of poetry with gifts of poetry books. When the children came, she took care of them so I could write, go to readings and perform. She put the magic of Emily Dickinson, Christina Rossetti and so many others into my life at a very young age, and set me on my path as a poet. For that, I can never thank her enough.

Terri Muuss: I would like to thank Rainer and Atticus, my constant teachers, and Matt Pasca who makes the impossible always feel very possible.

About the Editors:

Terri Muuss is a writer, performer, director, educator and social worker. Her poetry/prose one-woman show, *Anatomy of a Doll*, received grants from New York Foundation for the Arts and *Poets and Writers* and was named "Best Theater: Critics' Pick of the Week" by the *New York Daily News*; it has been performed throughout the US and Canada since 1998. Terri's poetry has appeared in *Bolts of Silk, Apercus Quarterly, Atticus Review, Long Island Quarterly, Brevity Poetry Review, Red River Review, Poetrybay Magazine, Paterson Literary Review, JB Stillwater's* online journal and four anthologies: *Whispers and Shouts: An Anthology of Women's Voices on Long Island* (2012), *Veils, Halos, and Shackles: International Poetry on the Abuse and Oppression of Women* (2015), The *Bards Annual (2013 & 2014)* and Great Weather for Media's *I Let Go the Stars in My Hand*. Her poem "Rialto Beach" won the 2013 Great Neck Poetry Prize and her first book, *Over Exposed* (JB Stillwater Publishing, 2013), was nominated for the 2014 Pushcart Prize in Poetry, as was her poem "Anniversary" in 2015 by *Atticus Review*. She has had non-fiction pieces published in *Behind Closed Doors, Eunoia Review* and *Down in the Dirt*. Terri also co-produced and hosted the monthly Manhattan poetry series *Poetry at the Pulse* for two years and currently co-hosts a popular monthly series in Bay Shore called *Second Saturdays at Cyrus*.

Terri received her BA in Theatre from Kean University, trained at the American Musical and Dramatic Academy in NYC, and studied for several years at Michael Howard Studios in NYC. Her numerous stage credits include performing in Ireland's West End in *The Taffetas* after touring it regionally. Terri also provided voiceovers for a number of Anime features, including *Battle Arena Toshinden* (Chris), *Iria—Zeiram the Animation* (Kai) and *The Heroic*

Legend of Arsland and has appeared in many industrial and instructional videos.

Terri has directed hundreds of performances featuring children and teenagers (both original and established plays) at schools throughout New York City and Long Island. She has also spent many years directing one-woman Off-Broadway and Off-Off-Broadway productions, including Deborah Ortiz's *Changing Violet* (Nominated for two IT Awards–Best Solo Performance and Best Performance Art piece), Veronica Golos' *A Bell Buried Deep* (from book of the same name that won the Roerich Poetry Prize and was nominated for a Pushcart), Athena Reich's rock opera *Athena Under Attack* (Toronto Fringe Festival and Producers Club in NYC), and Lisa Ramirez's *Exit Cuckoo* (63rd Street Y). Terri excels at adapting material for the stage, having done so for *Changing Violet* and *Lemon Meringue (TBG, NYC)*.

As a licensed social worker (MSW, Hunter College '02), Terri specializes in the use of the arts as a healing mechanism for trauma survivors and teaches a course at Rutgers University to social workers entitled *Youth Development Through the Written Arts*. Terri is also a motivational speaker and life coach who specializes in group work and addiction/abuse counseling. She has worked as a social worker at both GirlSpace in East Harlem and LICADD on Long Island. Terri served as Communications Coordinator for the Bay Shore School District, where she has won awards for her efforts in Public Relations. Currently, Terri is a school social worker where she lives on Long Island with her husband, writer Matt Pasca, and her two ginger-haired boys, Rainer and Atticus, former *Ellen Show* "Presidential Experts." She is thrilled to be co-editing GTA with her dear friend and poetry sister, M.J. Tenerelli. www.terrimuuss.com

M.J. Tenerelli is a poet and a legal writer. She has worked as an editor of trade magazines and textbooks for the cosmetology, cosmetics and fragrance industries in New York City. She currently writes legal briefs for a Social Security Disability law firm and hosts a monthly poetry reading for the Northport Arts Coalition in Northport, NY. Her poetry has appeared in several anthologies, including *Cat's Breath* and *Estrellas En El Fuego*, both by *Rogue Scholars Press*. Her poems have been published in a number of print and electronic journals, including *Poetrybay*, *The Feminist Wire*, *Alaska Quarterly Review*, *The Improper Hamptonian*, *Zuzu's Petals*, *The Mom Egg*, *Blue Fifth Review*, *Poetry Kit*, *Poetry Super Highway*, *Big City Lit* and *Parameter*. She is a former editor of the art and literary magazine *The Wormwood Press*. She is the crazy proud mother of the brilliant and talented Jack and Kate. She is extraordinarily honored to have been involved with bringing this important book to fruition.

About the Cover Artist:

Janine DiNatale is a creative director, fine artist, musician, and community advocate. In her primary position as creative director you will find her overseeing the content and design for a variety of clients. She has a passion for effective communication and enjoys the brainstorming process.

Janine's mother gave her full use of her art books and supplies which gave Janine the opportunity to become creative at a very early age. She started painting in oils and acrylics and developed a love for painting, sketching, and drawing as a young child. She attended art school and graduated with an Advertising Art and Design degree from SUNY Farmingdale and then furthered her studies at the School of Visual Arts in New York City. After working for a few years in local New York advertising agencies, she ventured on her own with the idea that she had a better chance of pay equality, and raising a family her way, if she were independent. She is now in her 27th year of being happily and successfully self-employed and has received over 20 awards from various competitions and institutions throughout her career.

Along with being an artist, Janine is also a vocalist, having performed professionally since the age of 16. Her multi-faceted talent has led her to various venues including solo concerts and studio recording dates. Janine has been headlining performances in the tri-state area for over a decade. Along with her favorite accompanists she has performed multiple sold out shows at the YMCA Boulton Center for the Performing Arts, and is a featured artist for the Islip Arts Council Free Concert Series. Her performances have also included a series at the famous Rainbow Room in New York City, along with performances at the Tilles Center with the "Glenn Miller Orchestra" and several concerts for the Oyster

Bay Distinguished Artists Series. Janine has also performed numerous times at Long Island's Winterfest, Jazz on the Vine.

Aside from art and music, she is an active community volunteer. Janine used her performance and marketing skills to create a program for AIDS Awareness (NY) titled "Remember AIDS", wherein she raised money for local non-profits in honor of her brother Frankie.

She also researched and designed a hands-on wellness program titled "Wellness Across America" that was implemented in schools both in NY and CT. Janine developed a 12-week intervention pilot program to help overweight children and their families, and a "Wellness Ambassadors" program for elementary schools that focused on overall well-being, not only including good nutrition and exercise, but also focusing on being kind to each other and the earth.

Janine has offered her time to many not-for-profits and various charities and community service committees: Glastonbury Education Fund (CT) Wellness Ambassadors (CT), Bay Shore Brightwaters COMPASS (NY), Bay Shore Schools Arts Education Fund (NY), Bay Shore Wellness Alliance (NY), and Bay Shore Summit Council and the Islip Arts Council (NY).

Born and raised on Long Island, DiNatale now resides in Connecticut with her loving husband and together they are raising three strong, loving and talented girls.

Contributor Biographies:

Sue Allen is a pediatric physical therapist and women's roller derby enthusiast. She began writing poetry in the fall of 2010 inspired by the warm and generous poetry community of Long Island. Her poems have appeared in the *Poets' Performance Association Literary Review*, and the *Perspectives II, Whispers and Shouts, Sounds of Solace, Bards Annual 2013* and *2014* anthologies, as well as the Princess Ronkonkoma Productions *Landscapes of Transition* exhibit.

Hala Alyan is a Palestinian-American poet and clinical psychologist whose work has appeared or is forthcoming in several journals, including *Third Coast, The Missouri Review* and *CALYX*. Her first full-length poetry collection, *Atrium*, was published by Three Rooms Press in New York City, and was awarded the 2013 Arab American Book Award in Poetry. Her second collection, *Four Cities*, was published by Black Lawrence Press in 2015. She resides in Manhattan.

Gabriella M. Belfiglio lives in Brooklyn, NY with her partner and three cats. She teaches self-defense, conflict resolution, karate, and tai chi to people of all ages throughout the five boroughs. Most recently, Gabriella won second place in the 2014 W.B. Yeats Poetry Contest. Gabriella's work has been published in many anthologies and journals including *VIA, E*ratio, Challenger International, Pinyon Review, Radius, The Centrifugal Eye, Folio, Avanti Popolo, Poetic Voices without Borders, C,C,&D, The Avocet, The Potomac Review, Eclectica, Lambda Literary Review, The Monterey Poetry Review* and *The Dream Catcher's Song*.

Maggie Berke is a 19-year-old student attending Bard College for Environmental Science with a concentration in gender and sexuality. She is interested in the intersection of feminism and environmentalism. She is a performance poet, as well as an actor and tuba player. Maggie is an alumnus of Bay Shore High School and the International Baccalaureate program. Her work can be found around open mic nights and in *The Writer's Block* as well as *Girls Get Busy*, a feminist art and poetry zine.

Maggie Bloomfield's poetry and essays have been published in *The Southampton Review (TSR), Long Island Sounds,* and *PoetryMagazine.com.* She was a staff lyricist for *Sesame Street,* winning an Emmy certificate, and has written lyrics extensively for the musical theatre in NYC. She recently graduated with an MFA from Stony Brook University, Southampton, where she was chosen as the Provost Student Lecturer in 2012, and served on the AWP panel, *Poetry as Object,* in 2013. As a psychotherapist/substance abuse counselor/poet, she is currently involved in *Poetry Street* in Riverhead, a movement to bring poetry into the community. She belongs to a group called *The Poets of Well-Being* along with two other poet/clinical social workers and they have been presenting a writing workshop called *Write for Your Life* in rehabs and schools. *The Poets of Well-Being* published a chapbook titled *The Poetry of Well-Being* and presented at both AWP 2015 and The Expressive Therapies Summit in NYC in 2014 with a focus that included their own journeys and which facilitated the healing power of the pen.

Sharon Bourke is a poet, painter and printmaker. She is of African-American heritage, was born in Brooklyn, New York some 86 years ago, and is still active in all of her artistic pursuits. Her poetry has appeared in *Poetry* magazine and numerous anthologies including *Understanding the New Black Poetry, Celebrations, Children of Promise, Songs of Seasoned Women, Long Island Sounds, Toward Forgiveness, Tamba Tupu: Africana Women's Poetic Self-Portrait,* and *Whispers and Shouts.* Her abstract and non-representational art can be found at *liblackartists.org/sharon_bourke.htm.*

Brooklyn-born **Barbara Ann Branca** has read original works on National Public Radio and featured at NYC's Cornelia Street Café, Bowery Poetry Club, Parkside Lounge, and Greenwich Village Bistro and on Long Island at libraries, cafes, the Huntington Poetry Barn, and Walt Whitman Birthplace, where she took first place in LI Poetry Collective's Super Poem Sunday 2010. Her work appears in *Polarity eMagazine* and the anthology, *Paumanok II*. As a science author and jazz singer, her poetry is creative nonfiction based on lifelong passions for music, heritage and the environment.

Meagan Brothers is the author of two novels for young adults, *Debbie Harry Sings in French* and *Supergirl Mixtapes*, both available from Henry Holt. Her latest novel, *Weird Girl and What's-His-Name*, was published in 2015 by Three Rooms Press. Her poetry has appeared most recently in *The Night Bomb Review* and on poetz.com. A native Carolinian, Meagan currently works and lives in New York City.

Teri Coyne is a writer, author, feminist and communicator. Teri primarily writes fiction and poetry and is the author of the novel *The Last Bridge* (Ballantine Trade Paperback, 2010). She is also a former stand-up comedienne who performed in clubs all over New York City. She is currently at work on her second novel and on her first collection of poetry. Teri holds a Bachelor of Fine Arts from New York University. She divides her time between New York City and the North Fork of Long Island. www.tericoyne.com

Jeanne Dickey's fiction and poetry has appeared in *Passages North*, *RE:AL*, *Karamu*, *Poet Lore*, and other journals. She is working on a short story collection and a novel.

Kate Boning Dickson is a wife, mother, musician, teacher and poet.

Lisa Freedman is a writer, teacher, and coach in NYC (http://lfwritingcoach.com/). Her work has appeared or is forthcoming in the *New York Times, Art & Understanding, POZ,* and *Satya Magazine.* She has also written for and performed with the AIDS Theatre Project. She received her MFA in Creative Writing from the New School.

Wendy Galgan is Chair and Associate Professor in the English Department at St. Francis College in Brooklyn, where she is also Director of the Women's Poetry Initiative, Co-Director of the Women's Center/Women's Studies Minor and Editor of *Assisi: An Online Journal of Arts & Letters.* Wendy's poetry won first and third prize in The Seacoast Writer's Association's 19th Annual Poetry Conference. Her poems have appeared in journals such as *California Quarterly* and *The AFCU Journal,* the website *On Earth As It Is,* and the online journal *Forge.* Her poem "Burning Angels: March 25, 1911" is in the anthology *Villanelles.*

Deborah Hauser is the author of *Ennui: From the Diagnostic and Statistical Field Guide of Feminine Disorders* (Finishing Line Press, 2011). She graduated from Stony Brook University with a Masters in English Literature. She has taught at Stony Brook University and Suffolk County Community College. Her poetry has been published in journals such as *The Wallace Stevens Journal, Dogwood,* and *Antiphon.* She is a contributing editor at *The Found Poetry Review.* She leads a double life on Long Island where she works in the insurance industry when she isn't writing poetry.

Gladys Henderson's poems are widely published and have been featured on PBS Channel 21 in their production, *Shoreline Sonata.* In 2010, she was named Walt Whitman Birthplace Poet of the Year. Finishing Line Press published her chapbook, *Eclipse of Heaven* in June 2008.

Vicki Iorio is a native Long Islander who thought she could escape this island and live elsewhere, but New York is in her heart and poetry keeps her heart beating.

Karen Jakubowski is a native Long Islander. Karen is a cancer survivor. She daylights as a paralegal in real estate. She can often be found in coffee shops or reading tarot. Karen is a Pushcart Prize nominee. Local Gems Press released her poetry collection *Scrawny Girl* in 2013 and released her chapbook of tarot poems, *Burned at the Stake,* in the spring of 2015. Her poetry has appeared in numerous on-line poetry journals and print anthologies.

Nancy Keating's work has been published in several anthologies, including *Whispers and Shouts, Long Island Sounds, Toward Forgiveness, Paumanok II, Writing Outside the Lines, Sounds of Solace, Freedom Verse, Perspectives,* and *Retail Woes,* as well as numerous literary magazines and webzines including *Iconoclast, Chaffin Review,* and *Long Island Quarterly.* She is the author of a volume of poems, *Always Looking Back,* and two chapbooks. A graduate of Bucknell University and the University of Minnesota, she lives on Long Island, New York with her poet husband, Tom Stock.

Kate Kelly is a visual artist and poet. She has presented her poetry at numerous venues and been published in many small press books. She has authored several chapbooks and a collection of poems, *Barking at Sunspots.* Her artwork has been widely exhibited regionally. She presently makes her home in Northport, NY, with her husband James Friel and her faithful four-legged companion, Leo.

Linda Kleinbub is a mentor at *Girls Write Now,* an organization that works with at-risk high school girls who have a passion for writing. Her work has appeared in *The New York Observer, Our Town - Downtown, Statement of Record, Short, Fast and Deadly* and *The Best American*

Poetry Blog. She received her MFA in Creative Writing from The New School. She holds a Masters in Library and Information Science and a Bachelor of Arts in Computer Science, both from Queens College (CUNY). She is a painter, photographer and organic gardener.

Mindy Kronenberg is an award-winning writer whose poetry, essays, and reviews have appeared in over 400 publications in the U.S. and abroad. Her writing accolades include film, video, and theater, and she has been featured in art installations. She teaches at SUNY Empire State College and offers workshops in the community through *Poets & Writers*, BOCES, and the Walt Whitman Birthplace. She edits *Book/Mark Quarterly Review* and is the author of *Dismantling the Playground* and *Images of America: Miller Place*.

Jane LeCroy is a NYC based poet, singer, performance artist (*Sister Spit*, *Vitapup*, *Nu Voices*, *Hydrogen Jukebox*, *Transmitting*) and mother of three. She fronts the avant-pop-post-punk band **The Icebergs** and has been published widely. Her chapbook, *Names (Booklyn)* was published as part of their award-winning ABC chapbook series and purchased by the Library of Congress along with her braid! In April 2013, *Three Rooms Press* released her first full-length collection, *Signature Play*, a multimedia book of lyrical poems, including musical scores and collage. Jane is a teaching artist in NY public schools.

Jennifer Magliano is a teacher, interfaith minister and freelance editor. She writes ceremonies, poetry, fiction, and essays, and enjoys experimenting with new genres. Her chapbook of poetry, *And You Were the Pole of the Planet*, was published in 1999. Last summer, Jennifer presented as a guest writer at Adelphi's Alice Hoffman Young Writers' Retreat. Now she shares her experiences rebuilding after

Superstorm Sandy in her blog *Our Old Normal*, and works with the very youngest of writers in her kindergarten class. Jennifer hopes to move back to her Long Beach home sometime this year, with her husband Steve and their dog Lucy.

Liv Mammone is a poet and future-novelist currently navigating the choppy sea of life after the MFA. She has studied and taught creative writing at Hofstra University and Queens College, and worked as an editor for American Book Publishing and PineRock Productions. Her work has appeared in *Wordgathering* and *Poetry and Performance* and is forthcoming in *Wicked Banshee* and *The Medical Journal of Australia*.

A nine-time Pushcart-Prize nominee and National Park Artist-in-Residence, **Karla Linn Merrifield** has had over 500 poems appear in dozens of journals and anthologies. She has eleven books to her credit, the newest of which is *Bunchberries, More Poems of Canada,* a sequel to *Godwit: Poems of Canada* (FootHills), which received the Eiseman Award for Poetry. Her poem "See: Love" was a finalist for the 2015 Pangaea Prize. She is assistant editor and poetry book reviewer for *The Centrifugal Eye*, a member of the board of directors of Just Poets (Rochester, NY), and a member of the New Mexico State Poetry Society, the Florida State Poetry Society and TallGrass Writers Guild. Visit her blog, *Vagabond Poet*, at *karlalinn.blogspot.com*.

Gloria g. Murray's poetry has been published in various journals including *The Paterson Review, Poet Lore, Bardic Echoes, Third Wednesday* and *The Ledge*, etc. Her poetry was honored by Ted Kooser in his on-line column *American Life in Poetry* and was featured in the *Newsday* column *On the Isle*, in October, 1995. She is the recipient of poetry awards from PPA, the Town of Great Neck and is the 2014 1st place winner of The Anna Davidson Rosenberg award from *Poetica Magazine*. She is a playwright as well and has had her one-act play performed at the Northport One-Act festival and off-Broadway.

Joan Vullo Obergh, from Seaford, New York, holds both an RN degree and a Masters in Counseling. Her background, which is often reflected in her writing, is in women's counseling, in addition to being a hotline crisis center volunteer. Joan is widely published and has earned ten first place poetry contest awards in the last ten years. *Rara Avis* is an autobiographical chapbook dating back to her first childhood poem. She also co-authored *Chapter One, An Anthology of Short Fiction*, with the group of talented prose writers she has facilitated for the last 12 years.

Stella Padnos-Shea's poems can be found in the *Chest* medical journal, *Yes, Poetry*, *Lapetitezine.com*, and *ldyprts.tumblr.com*, an online collaboration with jewelry artist Margaux Lange. In an early incarnation, one of her poems was nominated for a Pushcart Prize. Having been employed as a college English instructor, jewelry maker and therapist, she is presently embarked on her greatest and most challenging project yet: raising four-year-old daughter Mirabel. Her debut full-length collection of poetry, *In My Absence*, is forthcoming in 2016 from Winter Goose Publishing. You can email her at *Stella.Padnos@gmail.com* or genuinely in the artistic cliché of Brooklyn.

Harriet Pasca-Ortgies enjoyed working as a library media specialist in public education for 26 years – interacting with students, encouraging their curiosity for knowledge and helping their growing awareness of global issues. Since retiring, she is able to spend more time writing poetry and exploring art. She has fun playing with her grandchildren, loves creatures of all kinds, and finds gardening a form of meditation and joy. She is proud of her sons, both teachers: Matt, a poet and Jesse, an artist. Harriet is thankful for her husband, Harry, who is always encouraging her to spread her wings.

Kelly J. Powell is a poet from Long Island.

After **Anita S. Pulier** retired from practicing law in New York and New Jersey, she served for several years as the U.S. representative for the Women's International League for Peace and Freedom at the United Nations. She now serves on the board of The Jane Adams Peace Association. Her chapbooks *Perfect Diet* and *The Lovely Mundane* were published by Finishing Line Press. Anita's poems have appeared both online and in print in many journals including *Askew, Linnet's Wings, Riverbabble, Oberon, Your Daily Poem, Avalon Literary Review, Extracts, The Buddhist Poetry Review* and *The Los Angeles Times*.

R.A.K is a professional musician in NYC, who has music directed and/or played for well over 300 musicals and cabaret shows worldwide. She has also worked professionally as a magician, and is an amateur linguist, having formally studied four languages & learned expressions in many others. She holds B.A.s in Music and Slavic Linguistics, both from the University of Chicago.

Barbara Reiher-Meyers is a Long Island poet and former board member of the Long Island Poetry Collective and The North Sea Poetry Scene. She has facilitated monthly workshops, sends weekly emails about local poetry events, has coordinated events for the Northport Arts Coalition and Smithtown Township Arts Council, among others, and edited several volumes of poetry. Her poetry has been published in print journals and online. Her first book of poems is *Sounds Familiar*. You can email her at *reiherbpoet@optonline.net*

Emma Rose is a Shaman healer and a poet/story teller who uses story and tarot for the healing of ancient wounds, weaving mythological tapestries that celebrate the emerging feminine principle.

Stacy Santini is a Long Island poet and writer. She is CEO, Founder and Owner of The Poetry Connection, dedicated to bringing arts and cultural awareness to the elderly. She holds a Bachelor of Arts in English from Adelphi University. She is a member of Long Island's Performance Poet's Association. She worked with *Companion Star, A Living Laboratory for the Creative Process*. Stacy is currently working on a play regarding her experience and journey as a woman in today's culture. She is also a freelance feature writer and music journalist.

Wanda Schubmehl has written poetry since the age of 4. These early poems may be found in the blue-bound book with cut-out gold letters her mother made. Later work may be found in *Rattle, Redactions, The Centrifugal Eye,* and *Ghoti,* among others, and in a chapbook, *Schroedinger's Cat (*FootHills Publishing, 2011). Wanda lives in Rochester, NY, and curates the Genesee Reading Series for the literary center Writers and Books.

Karen Schulte is a retired Social Worker who, after a long hiatus, has returned to writing as an art. She has had her poetry published in several magazines such as the *The Avocet* and is featured in recent anthologies including *Whispers and Shouts, an Anthology of Poetry by Women of Long Island, Paumanok Interwoven* and *Bards Annual*, 2013 and 2014. She has won several prizes for her poetry, including East End Arts 2012, Great Neck Plaza Poetry Contest, 2013, and Princess Ronkonkoma, 2014. She is also an active member of Performance Poets of Long Island.

Iris N. Schwartz, a Pushcart Prize nominee for poetry, writes fiction, poetry, nonfiction, and drama. Her book of poetry with Madeline Artenberg, *Awakened*, was published by Rogue Scholars Press. Other work has been anthologized in such collections as *An Eye for an Eye Makes the Whole World Blind: Poets on 9/11;* and *Stirring Up a Storm: Tales of the Sensual, the Sexual, and the Erotic;* and has appeared in such journals as *Ducts, Pikeville Review, Vernacular, Ludlow Press, The November Third Club, The Wormwood Press* and *Writing Raw* and *NYSAI magazine.*

Linda Simone's award-winning poems are widely published, most recently in *Adanna Literary Journal* and the anthologies *Remember* (Four Point Press, 2014) and *Radical Dislocations* (Chupa Cabra House, 2014). She is honored to have a poem included in *The Crafty Poet*, by Diane Lockward (Wind Publications, 2013). Her second chapbook, *Archeology,* was selected for publication and released in August 2014 (Flutter Press). When she isn't working or writing poetry, she is exploring the wonders of watercolor. She recently relocated to San Antonio from her beloved New York City. www.lindasimone.com.

Starting out as a painter and printmaker, **Barbara Southard's** work evolved over the years into a combination of image and word. She currently serves on the editorial board of *Xanadu* and designs book covers for authors and literary magazines, including *Xanadu*. Over a span of time she has taught art enrichment to school children, worked with high-risk children at a mental health clinic, and currently teaches poetry to children at Walt Whitman Birthplace. Her work has been published in *Poet Lore, Long Island Quarterly, The Long Islander, Mobius, Boones Dock Review* and *Canary*, as well as several anthologies.

Dd. Spungin is a member of Poets in Nassau and Performance Poets Association and hosts monthly poetry readings for both organizations. Her poetry appears in print and on-line journals and poetry anthologies. She pens a monthly poem for Brave Hearts, the newsletter for St. Francis Hospital on Long Island, NY. Several of her poems have been set to music by NY composer, Julie Mandel.

Miriam Stanley is a NYC poet. Her books *Not to Be Believed*, *Get Over It*, and *Let's Fly to Trazodone* are published by Rogue Scholars Press. She also has two poems included in the *Occupy Wall Street* Anthology. She has performed in America and Israel.

Pramila Venkateswaran, poet laureate of Suffolk County, Long Island (2013-15), and author of *Thirtha* (Yuganta Press, 2002), *Behind Dark Waters* (Plain View Press, 2008), *Draw Me Inmost* (Stockport Flats, 2009), *Trace* (Finishing Line Press, 2011), and *Thirteen Days to Let Go* (Aldrich Press, 2015), is an award-winning poet who teaches English and Women's Studies at Nassau Community College in New York. Recently, she won the Local Gems Chapbook contest for her volume, *Slow Ripening*. Author of numerous essays on poetics as well as creative non-fiction, she is also the 2011 Walt Whitman Birthplace Association Long Island Poet of the Year. For more information, visit *www.pramilav.com*.

Muriel Harris Weinstein's poems are in many literary journals including *The Comstock Review, The Cortland Review, Elysian Fields, The Cape Rock, Freshette, The Nassau Review, Oberon* and *Xanadu*, as well as many anthologies. She also writes for children: *When Louis Armstrong Taught Me Scat*, a picture book on the joys of chewing bubble gum, won a Junior Library Guild award & the bio of Louis Armstrong's youth, *Play Louis, Play!* won 3 national awards, including the Paterson Prize, and was a nominee for the Texas Bluebonnet along with being published in Japanese. Her poetry chapbook, *What Women Will Do* was published by Finishing Line Press. She is currently working on *The Papyrus Papers*, a historical fiction book for young adults about the ancient liberated Queen Hatshepsut.

Michelle Whittaker is a poet and pianist. Her work has recently appeared in the *New Yorker, The Southampton Review, Vinyl Poetry, Drunken Boat, Great Weather for Media* and *Long Island Quarterly*. She has received a Jody Donahue Poetry Prize, a Pushcart Special Mention and a Cave Canem Fellowship.

Index

1

100 Rapes · 45

A

A Woman in My Poems · 75
Acorns · 63
Air & All the Elements · 8
Allen, Sue · 28
Alyan, Hala · 16, 51
Anniversary Ritual at Pinelawn · 15
At Night · 29

B

Baby Boom Room · 13
Because a Gig Was Hard to Come by in 1933 · 11
Belfiglio, Gabriella · 6
Berke, Maggie · 29
Bloomfield, Maggie · 70
Bourke, Sharon · 40
Branca, Barbara Ann · 13
Brothers, Meagan · 30
Bruised Fruit · 42

C

Caught In A Spider's Web · 41
Chapped Hands · 26
Coyne, Teri · 45
Crossing Over · 36

D

Dickey, Jeanne · 21
Dickson, Kate Boning · 12
Dina · 59

E

Edie · 34
Even Fevers Make Bodies · 16

F

Feng Shui in 13E · 71
Foreword · 5
Freedman, Lisa · 23

G

Galgan, Wendy · 32
God of the Spokes · 23

H

Hard Rain · 62
Hauser, Deborah · 60
Henderson, Gladys · 20

I

In April · 60
In Morocco · 3

Iorio, Vicki · 36
It Started · 57

J

Jakubowski, Karen · 42

K

Keating, Nancy · 73
Kelly, Kate · 62
Kleinbub, Linda · 19
Kronenberg, Mindy · 4

L

LeCroy, Jane · 22
Like that of the Purple Orchid in
   My Garden · 19
Lilith · 5
Listen, · 51
Location x 3 · 30
Lotus Feet · 28
love, lamp · 12
Lunch · 21

M

Magliano, Jennifer · 8
Mammone, Liv · 37
Merrifield, Karla Linn · 11
Mothers of the Dead Children
   Society · 54
Murray, Gloria g. · 65
Muuss, Terri · 68

O

Obergh, Joan Vullo · 15

P

Padnos-Shea, Stella · 57
Pasca-Ortgies, Harriet · 56
Penelope · 32
Penis Envy · 65
Polished Dimes · 68
Powell, Kelly J. · 66
Predator · 7
Pulier, Anita S. · 71

R

R.A.K · 61
Rara Avis · 27
Recovered Memory ABC's · 61
Reiher-Meyers, Barbara · 55
Rope Dancers · 20
Rose, Emma · 5

S

Salmonella Cinderella · 22
Santini, Stacy · 34
Schubmehl, Wanda · 63
Schulte, Karen · 53
Schwartz, Iris N. · 3
Sex · 70
Simone, Linda · 27
Southard, Barbara · 54
Spungin, Dd. · 26
Stained Glass Prison · 66
Stanley, Miriam · 59

T

Telling Our Stories · 53
Tenerelli, M.J. · 75
The Blind Date · 37
The Grammar of Higher Learning
   · 73

The Long Shadow of Evil · 47
The Rapist's Wife · 43
Thin Walls · 40

U

Unbecoming · 6

V

Veiled · 4

Venkateswaran, Pramila · 43, 47

W

Weinstein, Muriel Harris · 41
What is Left · 56
Whittaker, Michelle · 7

Y

Youngest of Seven · 55

Recent Releases

From JB Stillwater

Take Any Ship That Sails
Michele Heeney
ISBN: 978-1-937240-67-7
Genre: Poetry/American

This 5th book of Michele's spans 45 years of writing poems and thousands of miles of geography. It is a selection of poems from Michele's teen years in Pennsylvania to recent poems inspired by the beautiful mountains and Mesas of New Mexico. There are poems from Monterey and Marin counties, California. From times spent writing at Esalenin Big Sur. They cover nature, love, art, and personal growth. There are some of free verse and classical form.

Geographic: A Memoir of Time and Space
Miriam Sagan
ISBN: 978-1-937240-62-2
Genre: Personal Memoirs

Miriam Sagan has written a book that tells in poetic beauty the often difficult and frequently uplifting history of her own life and challenges as she tumbles through the mixture of events that helped contribute to the writer that she is today.

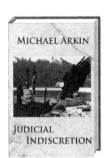

Judicial Indiscretion
Michael Arkin
ISBN: 978-1-937240-63-9
Genre: Fiction/Legal

The Santa Fe Trail sets the scene for drug running, money laundering, treachery, murder, and challenges to character, as **Judicial Indiscretion** plays out in the cactus-studded New Mexican Rio Grande Valley landscape. A highly respected judge is murdered in Mimbres County, New Mexico and local attorney David Madrid is arrested for the crime. San Diego Times investigative reporter Linda Lawson prevails upon long- time friend Matt Lucas to assist in the defense of David, her brother.

J.W. Valentine
Barbara Novack
ISBN: 978-1-937240-57-8
Genre: Young Adult, Coming of Age

Summer 1952, and fourteen-year-old J.W. Valentine wishes the world and everyone in it would leave him alone. His life so far has not gone well. His defenses – anger and cleverness – have only gotten him in trouble. And now the state has sent him to a farm for rehabilitation, something he is determined to resist. He finds in the nearby town resentment and suspicion and, out on the farm, Mac, a man who may know something of value, and Cassie, the girl who will haunt him for the rest of his life. Amid the distrust, there is discovery, and through it, J.W. Valentine tells a moving story of love.

All I Can Gather & Give
Patti Tana
ISBN: 978-1-937240-45-5
Genre: Poetry/Women Authors

All I Can Gather & Give is a book of seventy-five poems by Patti Tana that is composed of three sections: "The Ally You Have Chosen," "Imperfect Circles," and "Every Season Has Its Beauty." This ninth collection of poems is a tribute to the poet's sources of inspiration in nature and the people she loves. In a voice intimate and accessible, Tana finds words to transcend adversity and affirm a life that is passionately lived.

Over Exposed
Terri Muuss
ISBN: 978-1-937240-23-3
Genre: Poetry/Women Authors

In the pages that follow, Muuss brings us close to what we might describe as the secret war, the intimate war, which resides in closed rooms, in seemingly ordinary homes. Yet these poems are written, reader, with such delicacy, such concern for image, for pause, and purpose-for, in fact, beauty. Yes, these poems and prose pieces turn on the beauty of poetry, of what art can accomplish. I bid you open the book. It is a miracle. -- Veronica Golos

Something Like Life
Barbara Novack
ISBN: 978-1-937240-09-7
Genre: Poetry/Women Authors

In this neat and intelligent book of poetry *Something Like Life* author Barbara Novack describes the often subliminal messages that are sent to us every day in the beauty and sadness we often see around us in nature and human experience. This book is poetry at its best.

A Thousand Doors
Matt Pasca
ISBN: 978-0-984568-16-1
Genre: Poetry/American/General

Poet Matt Pasca explores how personal suffering can be transformed into grace, as if through alchemy, when that grief can be shared with others. Using the Buddhist "Mustard Seed" parable as scaffolding, Pasca's work pays homage to Kisa Gotami's quest to save her son by finding a home where, impossibly, no suffering has befallen the inhabitants.

CPSIA information can be obtained
at www.ICGtesting.com
Printed in the USA
FSOW04n0348280416
19772FS